Taking Charge of your Career

Revised Edition

by Leigh Bailey

The Bailey Consulting Group

Coaching and Consulting in Leadership, Team and Career Development
www.thebaileygroup.com

International Standard Book No. 0-9664664-1-1

Acknowledgements

There are many people I would like to thank for their help in writing this book. Thanks first to Maureen for your love, support and encouragement, and to Allison for your reminders to be an optimist.

Thank-you to Sharon, Doug, Sandra, Maureen, Nancy and Marnie for reviewing and editing the manuscript, and to Steve for turning the manuscript into a book.

Thank-you to all of the clients and colleagues with whom I have been privileged to work during the past 20 years. It is from that experience that this book was made possible.

Finally, thank-you to Ruth, without whose encouragement and wisdom I would never have made the commitment to myself to make this book a reality.

Acknowledgements for the Revised Edition

The reception that **Taking Charge of Your Career** has received since it was first published in 1998 has been very gratifying. The book has been used in workshops for employees and managers in large and small corporations throughout the United States, and as a textbook in both undergraduate and graduate curricula. In addition, **Taking Charge of Your Career** has been employed, with favorable results, by career coaches and counselors in a variety of professional settings.

I remain convinced that the ideas and exercises offered in this book are as valid today as they were when the book was first published. The new edition reflects changes that have been suggested by users since the first publication and offers resources that were not available when the first edition was completed.

I want to again thank all of my clients, both individuals and corporations, for the opportunity to do what I love for the past many years. I also again want to thank Ruth Hayden, who has been my mentor and role model and great supporter.

I want to thank my daughter Allison for her presence in my life. I love you!

Finally, I want to thank my wife and partner Maureen, whom I love and respect with my whole heart. You are teaching me how to partner, and I am grateful for the journey.

Table of Contents

Introduction

Old ways of thinking about why we work, and what creates meaning, motivation, and satisfaction at work, are no longer useful. In organizations where change is the only constant, where even the best performers can expect only modest pay increases, and where traditional career paths have disappeared, the only certainty is this: You must be willing to take responsibility for yourself in new and radical ways if you hope to experience the joy that results from recognizing and doing the work you were created to do.

This responsibility is not for the faint-hearted. It requires asking yourself difficult, often frustrating questions about what you wish to contribute to the world. It requires confronting and giving up cherished illusions about money, about someone else being responsible for your work satisfaction, and about discovering neat, clear answers that work for a lifetime.

Having said all of this, it is also true that now is an exciting time to be alive and in the work force. Opportunities exist for people who are clear about what they are looking for and who are willing to put in the hard work to do their part to realize their dreams.

The end result may not be exactly what you expected, but it will include increased maturity, self confidence, a sense of purpose, and perhaps if you are fortunate, even joy.

This workbook is about helping you to accept the responsibility of **Taking Charge of Your Career.**

by Leigh Bailey

Overview

Welcome to the **Taking Charge of Your Career** workbook!

The purpose of the **Taking Charge of Your Career** workbook is to provide you with practical tools, a road map, and support for making your current job more satisfying and for setting and accomplishing future career goals. By focusing on these objectives, you will become a more valuable contributor to your organization, and you will be happier and more satisfied with your life.

A consistent theme throughout the **Taking Charge of Your Career** workbook is that you are ultimately responsible for your career or job satisfaction. While it is in the best interest of organizations to support employees in this effort, you must do the work to define and create satisfying work for yourself.

Taking Charge of Your Career has proven to be a powerful catalyst for empowering individuals like you to create more satisfying work lives. If you commit yourself to participate fully in this effort, your reward will be renewed energy and new knowledge, new tools, and a plan for creating and maintaining work that brings you satisfaction and makes a contribution to the world.

Objectives

By completing the **Taking Charge of Your Career** workbook, you will:

- Gain a clearer understanding of what makes a job satisfying for you;

- Assess your satisfaction with your current job and develop specific plans for making your current job more satisfying;

- Learn and practice skills for setting and achieving longer term career objectives including identifying and researching possible future jobs, informational interviewing, and resume writing;

- Analyze your reactions to change and learn about key personal characteristics and skills required for creating change in your work life;

- Identify specific next steps for increasing your career and job satisfaction.

Creating Conditions for Success

To experience success in working through this workbook, you will need a partner. Trying to do it alone or trying to force yourself to make changes before you are ready will create stress and undermine your efforts to realize your goals.

Strategy #1: Find a friend or co-worker to partner with you in this effort. Ideally, your "partner" will be someone who is committed to working through this workbook for himself or herself. In this way, you can listen to, coach, and support each other along the way. Do not choose your spouse or another close family member as your partner. You want someone who does not have a strong opinion or personal "stake" about who you are or what you should be doing.

Strategy #2: Take some time now to reflect on what you hope to achieve by working through the **Taking Charge of Your Career** workbook. Being clear about and writing down your objectives significantly increases the likelihood that you will accomplish them, and will give you something to refer back to when your energy and motivation need a boost. Some typical goals might include:

- To know yourself better and to define what you want from your job or career;

- To better recognize whether or not a particular job is likely to be satisfying and a good "fit" for you;

- To identify and learn more about jobs that might interest you in the future;

- To get "unstuck" from a job that is no longer satisfying;

- To develop and implement strategies for making your current job more meaningful and satisfying;

- To prepare to respond to unexpected disruptions or opportunities in your work life.

Strategy #3: Set a reasonable, realistic deadline for completing the workbook, and write it in your calendar. Setting a reasonable deadline creates a little urgency, and keeps you moving on your work. Also, set some milestone deadlines for completing the various sections, and find ways to reward your progress.

A note of caution: When you are setting your deadline, keep in mind all of the other commitments that already exist in your life. Be realistic, and treat your deadlines as check-in points, and not opportunities to criticize yourself if you need to make adjustments.

Also, keep in mind that new insights may occur when you are on vacation, or exercising, or working on something else, so give yourself time and space for this to occur.

A reasonable objective might be to complete the workbook in six to eight weeks. You can adjust this later if necessary.

Strategy #4: Finding a regular time for you and your partners to meet will make scheduling easier and make your meetings more likely to occur. Pick a regular day and time to meet, and stick to it if at all possible.

On the Goals Worksheet on the next page, write two or three sentences summarizing your goal(s) for completing this workbook. Also, jot down the names of two possible partners, and set a date by which you will ask them about partnering with you. Finally, set an initial deadline for completing the workbook.

Goals Worksheet

Directions: Please complete the following statement as specifically as possible:

*What I want to accomplish by completing the **Taking Charge of Your Career** workbook is . . .*

1.

2.

3.

I would like to have at least one of the following people partner with me . . .

1.

2.

3.

I will ask them by (date):

My deadline for completing the workbook is:

Workbook Organization

The **Taking Charge of Your Career** workbook is organized in sections:

Section 1:	Career Fundamentals	Focuses on basic principles for personal and career development
Section 2:	Learning About Your Work Self	Exercises and resources for exploring your goals, values, skills, and interests
Section 3:	Individual Development Planning	Strategies for career management and increased satisfaction and effectiveness in your current job
Section 4:	Planning for Your Future	Identifying future career goals and strategies for accomplishing your goals (includes tips for informational interviewing and resume writing)
Section 5:	The Challenge of Change	Strategies for self-motivation and overcoming resistance to acting in new ways
Section 6:	Appendix: Guide for Facilitators and Career Coaches	A guide to the **Taking Charge of Your Career** workshop and using the workbook for career coaching

Begin *Section 1: Career Fundamentals* by reading and analyzing a case study about an employee named Mary, and some of the challenges she faces in her job and career planning. As you read, see if you recognize yourself in any of Mary's dilemmas.

Section 1

Career Fundamentals

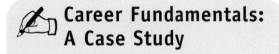

Career Fundamentals: A Case Study

Directions: Read the case study, answer the questions that follow, and then discuss your answers with your partner.

Mary has been in her current job for several years. She was very excited when she was first hired, and though she still basically likes what she is doing, Mary is finding it harder to "stay motivated" and do the quality work she expects from herself.

Much has happened at her company since Mary was hired. Two years ago, the company went through "downsizing" because of poor financial performance and because the company needed to operate more efficiently to survive. Though Mary is in no immediate danger of losing her job, top management has made it clear that seeking efficiencies and cutting out unprofitable lines of business is a permanent strategy.

Another unwelcome reality for Mary has been the "slowdown" in pay raises in recent years. The average annual pay raise for employees of her company is around 3%, and this also seems to be true of the companies where her friends work. At a party last Friday night, one of Mary's friends commented, "I better figure out another way to make my job satisfying, because I sure can't count on a big raise any more."

As if all the changes in the company weren't enough, Mary is also starting to notice a change in herself. She is not as excited about her work as she once was. Parts of her job which she once found exciting now seem routine and boring. The days pass much more slowly than they used to.

Mary has started to do some serious thinking about her future. She has considered going back to school, but isn't sure if that is what she really wants or what she would study. She has thought about finding a new job, but isn't sure where to begin. Mary is just not sure what to do . . . .

What parts of Mary's story remind you of your own job/career situation?

What might be some consequences to Mary if she does nothing about her current situation?

If you had to assign the responsibility for improving Mary's job satisfaction, what percentage would you give to Mary? Her employer?

What opportunities does this uncomfortable time offer for Mary?

Section 1: Career Fundamentals

Mary's situation illustrates several challenges that all employees face in creating and sustaining satisfying careers in today's world. The first is uncertainty. Downsizing and other strategies intended to make organizations more efficient make clear that you must be prepared for sudden changes in your work life, including the possibility of needing to find a new job.

The second challenge is the need to find meaning in your work in new ways. Pay raises and promotions have been primary tools used by organizations as incentives and for career enrichment. However, as organizations flatten out and move to teams, fewer promotions are available. Also, in recent years, the average annual increase in wages in the U.S. has been 3-4% — hardly enough to keep up with inflation, and certainly not enough to make any noticeable difference in an employee's lifestyle.

The third challenge is that all jobs become routine after awhile. In order to remain fresh and challenged, you must find ways to continue to learn and grow in your work.

You were probably able to empathize with at least some of the concerns that the case study about Mary raised. The case also raised some important questions. The answers to questions like: "Who is responsible for your job satisfaction?" and "What are the characteristics of satisfying jobs?" and "What are the steps to take to create and sustain satisfying work?" are fundamental and the focus of the next session.

Who is responsible?

"If you were to divide up 100% responsibility for your career satisfaction between you and your organization, how would you do it?" This question often sparks lively debate. Many will argue that their employer has 50% or more of the responsibility for employee satisfaction.

Unfortunately, there are several major problems with this argument. The first and biggest problem is that you are the only person who can discover what makes work satisfying for you! Your employer can't tell you what you value most from work, or what skills you most like to use, or what interests you most. You have to do the hard work of answering those questions.

Second, the hard reality is that your stake in your work satisfaction is greater than your employer's. Enlightened employers know that there is a strong relationship between "engaged" employees (employees who are challenged to use their talents and to continue to grow in their jobs) and business results such as employee retention, productivity, quality, and profitability. However, while your employer benefits from being fully committed to your development, you must take ultimate responsibility. In the competitive global economy in which we operate, you need to look out for your own best interests. That means discovering ways that you can add value as an employee and find satisfaction in the process. It is simply not an option to wait for your employer to manage your career for you.

This does not mean that your employer does not have a role in supporting your career satisfaction. Communicating about job opportunities, supporting employees' growth and development, and rewarding employees' contributions are all important ways your employer can support your career development. But you must set your own career goals and provide the energy and determination to accomplish them. This workbook is designed to show you how to do that.

Characteristics of satisfying jobs

Since each of us is unique, each will define satisfying work differently. However, there are some characteristics of satisfying work that seem to apply to almost everyone. People who like their work usually say:

- I know that I am good at my work.

- I think my work is important, and it fits with my values.

- I use my favorite and best skills in my work.

- I am interested in my work.

- I take charge of my goals and satisfaction in my work (and my life).

These characteristics describe the "non-monetary" rewards we get from work. These include self-esteem, a sense of purpose, enjoyment (fun!), and a feeling of having some control in life. Without these non-monetary rewards, even a job with good pay and benefits may start to feel more like a trap than something for which to feel grateful.

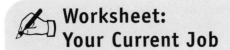

Worksheet: Your Current Job

Directions: Take a minute to answer the following questions, and then discuss your answers with your partner(s):

Which of the five characteristics of satisfying jobs are found in your current job? How?

Which of the five characteristics are not present in your current job?

How does this lack of satisfaction affect how you think and feel about your job? Yourself?

You may have noticed that even though these characteristics are common to almost everyone, they still will mean different things to different people. For example, you and your partner probably have different favorite skills. You probably also have different interests. For that reason, in order to make your current job more satisfying and to set future career goals, you will need to spend time thinking, writing, and talking about your unique skills, talents, interests, values, and needs. This will be the focus of *Section 2: Learning About Your Work Self,* which begins on the next page.

Section 2

Learning About Your Work Self

Section 2:
Learning About Your
Work Self

What does job satisfaction mean to you?

In *The Tao of Pooh*, by Benjamin Hoff, Winnie-the-Pooh asks the question, "How can you get very far, if you don't know Who You Are?" While you might not think of Winnie-the-Pooh as an expert in career development, his question sounds very much like one a career coach might ask.

In order to increase your work satisfaction, you need to "walk through" a series of steps. Clients who are successful in increasing their satisfaction usually follow this or a very similar process. The first step is to explore your educational background and work history to become more conscious about the decisions you've made, your reasons for making those decisions, and how your past decisions have brought you to your current (or most recent) job.

The next step is to become more aware of how you would describe, in Richard Bolles' words, "Your Ideal Job or Next Career." The purpose at this stage is not to "name" that ideal job or next career, but rather to identify what specific characteristics will make a job or career satisfying for you. Some specific areas to explore include:

- Your values;

- Your transferable skills;

- Your interests;

- Other specific characteristics (or needs) including how much money you require, the type of people you like to work with, your ideal work environment, the schedule you want to work, etc.

The following pages provide you with a number of exercises to start to find answers to these questions. You will also be referred to other resources for doing more in-depth work in these areas.

A word of caution is in order at this point. The work of trying to understand what satisfying work means to you is really the work of a lifetime. You will need to do some hard work to answer these questions as best you can, but don't drive yourself crazy trying to come up with "the perfect" answer.

Also, don't do this work alone. This is a time to really lean on the partner(s) you have chosen. Talk to each other on the telephone. Go to lunch with each other. Talking about your values, skills, interests, and needs will help to clarify them, and will also help you to get fresh outside perspectives. Best of all, you won't feel quite so alone.

Career Aspirations Dialogue

There is a saying which, paraphrased, goes something like: "Life is lived forward, but can only be understood backwards."

This is certainly true about a career. The choices you make today impact your future. However, making effective choices that lead to satisfaction requires looking back (reflecting) on your career and life so far for clues and patterns about your skills and talents, interests, goals, and desires.

The next exercise is designed to help you to reflect meaningfully on your career. It requires you to describe some of the career choices you have made so far and the reasons for your choices. It also asks you to reflect on and begin to articulate what you want from your career today and in the future.

This exercise should be a dialogue, or a conversation. Much of the power of the exercise comes from talking about yourself to a partner and being open to the questions your partner asks. Talking about yourself to someone else forces you to get your thoughts out of your head and into the world where you and your partner can examine them more objectively. This may sound a little scary, but this is one of the most powerful exercises in the workbook. And, speaking very practically, the ability to talk about yourself is crucial for seeking new career opportunities.

You may be tempted, for any number of reasons, to just sit and write your answers to the questions. Please resist this temptation. You will learn much more — and have more fun — if you have a partner ask you the questions and write your responses in your book for you.

Career Aspirations Dialogue

Directions: Give your workbook to your partner. Starting with the first question, your partner should ask each question and write your responses in your book. If your answer to a question raises another question, your partner should go ahead and ask it.

If both you and your partner are completing the exercise, you can either alternate asking each other each question (e.g. first you answer question #1, then your partner answers question #1, etc.) or one of you can ask the other all of the questions, and then switch.

1. Briefly describe each job you have had at your current place of employment. How long have you worked for your current employer?

2. Briefly describe your prior jobs.

3. As you look back over your career so far, what aspects of your jobs have you most enjoyed? What made them enjoyable?

4. Were there aspects of your jobs you especially disliked? Why were they disagreeable?

5. Did you choose your career or did it choose you? Explain.

6. On what areas of study did you concentrate in school? Why did you choose those areas? What additional education are you interested in pursuing, considering?

7. What talents do people who know you well identify in you . . . say you are naturally good at?

8. What are your major interests? What do you do for fun?

9. What are your professional ambitions or long-range goals? Personal goals?

10. How do you cope with change in your work life? In your personal life? What patterns do you see in how you cope with change?

11. What is your definition of success?

 **Reflection**

Directions: Now that you have completed the Career Aspirations Dialogue, it is time for some reflection. Grab a cup of coffee, tea or whatever helps put you in the mood for quiet thinking, and take some time to summarize your learnings about yourself from the aspirations dialogue. When you think about yourself in the future, what do you see? What would you really like to be doing? What would be fun to learn more about?

Write, draw a picture, write a poem — whatever will create a record of what you learned. When you finish, share your learnings with your partner.

Why do you work?

Why did you choose your current job? What makes your work satisfying? Why do you work at all?

The first and most obvious answer to the above questions is "To pay the bills." No doubt, one of the reasons most people work is the necessity of supporting themselves financially. But is that the only reason?

A manufacturing organization has a reputation for paying its employees very well. Employees of this organization talk of driving their new trucks and other "toys." Yet, these same employees also talk about feeling trapped because they are bored or unhappy with their jobs, but feel they cannot afford to leave because of the pay-cut they'd have to take.

An interesting question to ask is, "What, besides a paycheck, would be missing from my life if I did not have my current job?" Some possible answers could include important friendships, the satisfaction of feeling really competent at something, the opportunity to be of service to others, or the opportunity to lead others.

The point is, for most people, money alone does not provide job satisfaction. There are other needs that must be satisfied if work is to be fulfilling. These needs are related to a concept we call **values**.

Values Clarification

"What I really want is to spend more time with my children. They are just starting school, and I want to put them on the bus in the morning and be there when they come home from school in the afternoon. I think I might even want to have one more child. But I know I have to work too. My income is important to our family. How can I make this all work?"

Values are principles that have worth just because they are important to you. Values include principles like creativity, independence, economic security, helping others, physical health, change and variety, family happiness, and many others.

Each of us has a different set of values, or a different ranking of values, depending on our personality, our culture of origin, our spiritual beliefs, our current life circumstances, and other factors. For the person in the story described above, needs and desires surrounding her family have a large impact on her wants and needs from her work. You may share some of her wants and needs, or yours may be entirely different.

Knowing your values and striving to implement them, both at work and in your personal life, is crucial to your happiness. If your work is in harmony with your values, and provides opportunities to implement them, you are likely to find satisfaction in your job. If not, you are likely to feel frustration and a nagging sense that there is something else you should be doing.

It is interesting to note that while the importance of our values seems to remain quite consistent throughout our lives, the urgency we feel about particular values can change, depending on our circumstances. A good example is economic security. Even if economic security is really important to me, as long as I feel my income is secure, I am not likely to pay much attention to getting my needs satisfied in this area. However, if my economic security is suddenly threatened, the need to satisfy this value may become very intense.

Another example is values related to "family." Starting a family, for example, may intensify your need to satisfy values regarding time, freedom and flexibility that were previously less of an issue.

What Are Your Values?

Starting on the next page, you will be working on exercises designed to help you clarify your values, and the extent to which they are or are not being satisfied in your work.

✏️ Writing Stories

"When I was in college, I was the lead golf instructor for the city. I taught weekly classes to adults on the fundamentals of the game, and at the end of the six-week sessions we went and played a round of golf together. I also taught golf lessons to sixth-graders during the summer.

"This job involved several parts. Each week, I had to design a lesson plan. I would provide instruction to the whole class, and then work one-to-one with the adults to apply the skills I'd presented.

"I really enjoyed putting together the lesson plans and helping the adults. It felt really good to see my students start to have some success.

"The kids were harder. I felt like I was mostly babysitting and trying to keep them from hurting each other. I didn't like that as well."

A technique to help you recognize your most important values is to recall "peak experiences," and then analyze the stories for clues about your values. These same stories can also be used to identify your skills and talents.

Directions: On the following three pages, write or draw three brief "stories" from your life (the golf lessons example given above may be helpful in giving you a sense for how long the stories need to be and the type of information to include). Each story should describe an experience in your life when, either by yourself or working with others:

- You did something (e.g. participated in a high school musical, coached a basketball team, participated in a project at work, etc.)

- The "doing" caused you to feel alive, happy, productive; you felt you were really accomplishing something; you were in touch with your best self.

To get different perspectives on yourself, each of the stories should be from a different time or part of your life (work, outside of work, childhood).

When you have finished your stories, tell them to your partner. See what else you remember when you tell the story and what surfaces from your partner's questions.

 **Story #1**

A Work Example (Choose something from your current position or a previous job during your adult life.)

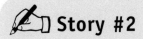 **Story #2**

An Example From Outside of Work (This might be a volunteering experience, a recreational experience, etc.)

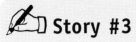

A Story From Your Childhood (1-18 years of age)

Values Clarification Exercise #1

Directions: Use your stories and the list of values on the next two pages to identify your most important values. To do this, read through each of your stories and identify 5-7 values that played a part in each story. For example, in the story about teaching golf lessons described above, some values might include helpfulness, achievement, expertness, pleasure, responsibility, and challenge.

After you have identified the values for each story, see if you can pick out 7-8 values that are most important to you. These will probably be values that appear in two or all three of your stories.

Once you identify your top 7-8 values, prioritize them (only your top 7-8 values): #1 is most important, #2 is second most important, etc. through #8.

Values From Story #1

1. _____
2. _____
3. _____
4. _____
5. _____
6. _____
7. _____

Values From Story #2

1. _____
2. _____
3. _____
4. _____
5. _____
6. _____
7. _____

Values From Story #3

1. _____
2. _____
3. _____
4. _____
5. _____
6. _____
7. _____

Most Important Values

1. _____
2. _____
3. _____
4. _____

5. _____
6. _____
7. _____
8. _____

Values Definitions

Achievement	An accomplishment or success
Advancement	Upward movement in a chosen profession
Adventure	New and exciting challenges
Affection	Being loved and cared for; loving and caring for others
Artistic Creativity	Engage in creative work in any of several art forms (e.g. writing, sculpting, painting)
Challenge	Working on new problems; difficult tasks
Change and variety	Work responsibilities which frequently change in content or setting
Comfort	Physical ease; lack of stress
Competition	Being in a win/lose situation
Control	Being in charge; knowing what an outcome will be
Creativity (general)	Create new ideas, programs, or anything else not following a format previously developed by others
Directness	Speaking out; saying what's on your mind
Economic Security	No financial worries
Expertness	Being seen as knowledgeable; well regarded in your field
Fairness	Giving everyone an equal chance
Family Happiness	Balancing work and family needs
Friendship	Close relationships with others
Harmony	Lack of conflict or discord
Health	Physical and mental well-being
Helpfulness	Assisting clients and coworkers
Helping Society	Doing something to contribute to the betterment of the world
Independence	Having control of your own behavior (autonomy)
Influence people	Being in a position to change attitudes or opinions of other people
Inner harmony	Being at peace with yourself
Integrity	Acting according to your beliefs
Make decisions	Having the power to decide courses of action, policies, etc.
Moral fulfillment	Feeling that my work is contributing to a set of moral standards I believe are important
Personal development	Use of potential
Pleasure	Fun, laughs
Power	Control, authority over others
Profit/gain	Becoming wealthy
Recognition	Acknowledgment from others
Religious/Spiritual beliefs	Sustaining faith in a higher power
Responsibility	Accountable for outcomes

Risk	Element of danger, excitement
Stability	Knowing what will happen next; no surprises
Supervision	A position involving overseeing work done by others
Time freedom	Working according to my own time schedule; no set hours
Tradition	Customs; a link with the past
Wisdom	Understanding life
Work alone	Doing projects by myself, without significant contact with others
Work with others	Having close working relationships with a group; working as a team toward common goals

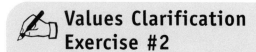

Values Clarification Exercise #2

Directions: For your five most important values (#1-5) on page 27:

1. How well are your top values being satisfied in your current job? Give examples.

2. Which of these values, if it (they) were to be better satisfied, holds the greatest potential for increasing your work satisfaction? Explain.

3. What ideas do you have to increase your level of satisfaction with the value(s) you selected in question 2? What ideas does (do) your partner(s) have?

Skills and Talents

Allison has had many different jobs in her career. She started out as a customer service representative at a financial institution. Some of her responsibilities included helping customers over the telephone and providing training to other bank employees.

Later, she was promoted to a supervisory position, and had responsibility for leading a staff of customer service and sales people.

Eventually, Allison was invited to join the training and development staff in her bank and had responsibility for training managers and salespeople throughout the organization.

Part of what makes a job satisfying is the opportunity to use your skills and talents. **Skills** are abilities that you have **learned** to do well. **Talents** are your **natural** endowments, abilities that are "part of you," that people say you're a "natural" at, and that you may overlook because they come so easily to you. Usually, talents are also abilities that you enjoy using, that bring you satisfaction.

In the example given above, some of Allison's talents include the ability to communicate with others, the ability to teach, the ability to establish helping relationships, and the ability to solve problems. Through experience, Allison has become even more adept at using her talents, and also developed skills at supervising others and selling.

The clearer you are about your skills and talents, the more directly you can seek opportunities in your current job to better use your skills and talents, and to recognize other jobs that you might enjoy because they offer the opportunity to use your skills and talents.

The following exercises are designed to help you identify your skills and talents, both from your perspective and through the input of others whose opinions you value.

Skills and Talents Exercise #1

Transferable skills are those which can be used in a variety of different jobs. Examples include skills such as selling, writing, organizing, and communicating with others.

In each of your jobs, you apply your transferable skills in a particular way. For example, if you are a banker, you apply selling, numerical, and counseling skills to help customers meet their financial objectives. Those same skills could also be applied to selling shoes or running a training and development consulting business.

This mindset is critical to survival in a changing economy. Instead of thinking of yourself as a job title, think of yourself as a bundle of transferable skills that, with the required knowledge and experience, can be applied in many different ways.

Directions: Read through the stories you wrote for the values exercises (pages 23-25) and identify transferable skills and abilities from the list below that you demonstrated in each story. For example, if one of the stories you wrote is about being a member of a project team, you might identify skills such as persuading, negotiating, or meeting deadlines. Use the worksheet on the next page to capture the skills you identify in each story, and to note your favorite skills and abilities.

Skills and Abilities List

Adaptable to changing situations	Facilitating	Mentoring
Aesthetically sensitive	Expertise with computers	Negotiating
Analyzing problems	Flexibility	Observing accurately
Assessing resources	Having fun	Organizing/planning
Attention to detail	Imagination with ideas	Persuading
Coaching	Imagination with things	Physical stamina
Collecting information	Interpreting data	Precision
Concentration/focus	Learning new skills	Public speaking
Coordinating project/tasks	Maintaining systems	Research
Counseling	Making decisions	Resolving conflicts
Critiquing	Managing	Seeing possibilities
Developing prototypes	Managing crises	Selling
Disciplining fairly	Manual dexterity	Solving quantitative problems
Establishing procedures/rules	Meeting deadlines	Strategizing
	Meeting people easily	

Supervising others
Synthesizing information
Talking
Teaching

Understanding complex
    ideas
Understanding how
    tools/machinery work

Working on a team
Working with numbers
Working with theories
Writing

Skills and Abilities
From Story #1

1. _____

2. _____

3. _____

4. _____

5. _____

6. _____

7. _____

Skills and Abilities
From Story #2

1. _____

2. _____

3. _____

4. _____

5. _____

6. _____

7. _____

Skills and Abilities
From Story #3

1. _____

2. _____

3. _____

4. _____

5. _____

6. _____

7. _____

Your Favorite Skills and Abilities

1. _____

2. _____

3. _____

4. _____

5. _____

6. _____

7. _____

8. _____

Skills and Talents
Exercise #2

Using your *talents* or natural gifts is a vitally important component of your career satisfaction. When you are using your gifts, you are likely to feel energized, competent, and excited about your work. Think about something you do really well and that comes easily to you. This could be anything from working with numbers, to teaching, to working with computers. Chances are, when you are engaged in this activity, you feel good about yourself and time passes very quickly.

On the other hand, think about a part of your work that you don't do as well and that you really struggle with, no matter how hard you try. This type of experience may be discouraging, and time can seem to crawl. In the same way, when you are in a job that does not utilize your gifts, you are likely to feel tired, inadequate, and frustrated.

Directions: People who know you well can help you identify talents whose importance you may minimize or those you are unclear about.

Your task in this exercise is to select three people ("Talent Scouts") who know you well, whose opinion you respect, and who you know will be honest with you.

Set up a time to meet with each of the three people you selected. Describe the definition of a talent and ask them what they think your top 4-5 talents are and how they have seen you use the talents they select. Write their answer on the following pages.

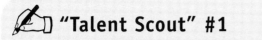 **"Talent Scout" #1**

Talent #1: _____

Examples:

Talent #2: _____

Examples:

Talent #3: _____

Examples:

Talent #4: _____

Examples:

Talent #5: _____

Examples:

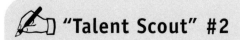 **"Talent Scout" #2**

Talent #1: _____

Examples:

Talent #2: _____

Examples:

Talent #3: _____

Examples:

Talent #4: _____

Examples:

Talent #5: _____

Examples:

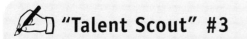 **"Talent Scout" #3**

Talent #1: _____

Examples:

Talent #2: _____

Examples:

Talent #3: _____

Examples:

Talent #4: _____

Examples:

Talent #5: _____

Examples:

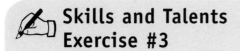

Skills and Talents
Exercise #3

Directions: In this exercise you will write a letter to your partner. Use the letter, which should be no longer than two typed pages, to describe the results of Skills Exercises #1 and #2. As you write this letter, think about these questions: How are the results of the two exercises similar? How are they different? What skills and talents do you most enjoy using? How could the skills and talents you enjoy help you to contribute to making the world better? What are you feeling in your body as you write the letter? What is your emotional reaction?

✍ What Are Your Interests?

Part of what makes work satisfying and rewarding is the opportunity to learn about and be involved with ideas and objects that interest you, that capture your attention. To become more consciously aware of your interests, reflect on the types of things you have spent your time studying and working on in the past, and what you are drawn to learning more about now and in the future.

Directions: As a way to start to become more aware of your interests, please answer the following questions:

1. *On what areas of study did you concentrate in school? How do you feel now about having chosen those areas?*

2. *What areas of study are you currently pursuing or considering pursuing?*

3. *What do you spend time learning about in your spare time, just for enjoyment?*

4. *What magazines, articles, books, television shows are you drawn to because you find them interesting?*

5. *As you look at your work life, can you think of times that you really enjoyed the work itself — the content? What specifically did you enjoy about it?*

6. *Who do you admire? Who are your heros? (Often, we see a part of ourselves in those we admire.)*

Beyond Values, Skills and Interests

Directions: The exercises that you have now completed were designed to help you clarify your values, skills, and interests. In addition to these, however, there are other things to consider when defining what work satisfaction means to you. Before you finish this section, write your answers to the following questions:

1. In what type of environment would you prefer to work? (e.g. in a city, in a large office building, in a small office building with a view of nature, mostly alone, mostly with other people, etc.)

2. How much money do you need to make to live a lifestyle that provides for your basic needs plus some of the pleasures that are important to you in life?

3. How do you want your work to contribute to the world? (e.g. helping people, improving the environment, making technical discoveries, improving understanding between people, etc.?)

4. What kinds of people would you like to work with as co-workers? As customers?

Other Resources

Many resources are available which help people to understand what they want from their work and what the world wants from them through their work. Some of the best include:

- *Whistle While You Work*, by Richard Leider and David Shapiro

- *Do What You Are*, by Paul Tieger and Barbara Barron-Tieger

- *The Inventurers*, by Janet Hagberg and Richard Leider

- *The New Quick Job Hunting Map*, by Richard Bolles

Psychological Assessments

Career professionals use a variety of assessment tools to assist individuals in making career choices. Two of the most widely used are the Myers-Briggs Type Indicator (MBTI)® and the Strong Interest Inventory.™ These tools can be very helpful for understanding what is important for you in a job to feel satisfied and to do your best work.

If you have never taken either of these assessment tools, check with your company's Human Resources department to see if there is someone in your organization who is qualified to administer these tools to you. If not, a local college or university or career organization may have people on staff who can administer the assessments.

If you want to learn more about the MBTI and how it relates to your career satisfaction, two wonderful resources are:

- *Do What You Are*, by Paul Tieger and Barbara Barron-Tieger

- *LifeTypes*, by Sandra Hirsh and Jean Kummerow

These books describe the MBTI in detail, and provide information about the characteristics of satisfying jobs for each "type"and the specific careers that individuals of each type commonly prefer.

Next Steps

Now that you have finished Section 2, you can probably do a good job of describing the characteristics that need to be present in a job if it is to be satisfying for you. In the next section, we will be using this information to identify ways to make your current job more satisfying. We will also use this information in *Section 4: Planning For Your Future.*

Section 3

Assessing Your Current Job

Section 3:
Assessing Your
Current Job

As you clarify what makes a job satisfying for you, a logical next step is to analyze your current job, both to assess your current satisfaction level and to better understand what parts of the job are a good "fit" for you and what parts fit less well.

In this section of the **Taking Charge of Your Career** Workbook, you will assess your current job against the values, skills, interests, and other needs you identified in Section 2. You will begin by learning about the process of change that seems to underlie all jobs and careers, and how to understand some of your feelings, both positive and negative, about your job.

Then, you will identify specific strategies for increasing your satisfaction and effectiveness in your current job, and begin to implement an individual development plan focused on better using your talents, upgrading skills you find fun and interesting, and defining specific actions for enhancing your overall life satisfaction.

The Life of a Job

In their book, *The Inventurers*, Janet Hagberg and Richard Leider suggest that all jobs follow a predictable pattern of change, or "life." This pattern is similar to the maturing process that you can observe in the development of a close relationship, or in the life of a new business.

Employees who are **new to a job** often go through a period of excitement, challenge, new learning, and anxiety as they build new relationships, acquire new skills, and strive to become productive in their new responsibilities. After a while, some of the **"newness" wears off**, and there is a period where the employee is productive, challenged, and, for the most part, satisfied despite the occasional frustrations that are part of any job.

Eventually, and inevitably, parts of the job that were originally challenging and interesting start to become **boring and routine**. Tasks that once provided excitement now provoke a "been there, done that" feeling. This period of "routine-ness" or "plateau" may provide a comfortable "resting point" for awhile, but eventually most people (though not all) reach a point where the boredom becomes too uncomfortable to ignore.

In general, there are three potential solutions for getting off the plateau:

- **Changing Careers:** This involves starting an entirely new career (e.g. a manager becoming a psychologist). It may require going back to school, and starting at a lower entry level in the new occupation. This is the most difficult option, and can take up to several years when new schooling is required. It takes energy, and persistence, and often (though certainly not always) is associated with life transitions which take place in the early to mid-thirties and late forties to early fifties, or by other significant life events (e.g. being fired from a job).

- **Changing Jobs:** This option still involves a new job, but the new job is in the same career as the previous job. Changing jobs may involve either the same organization, or going to work for a new organization. Hagberg and Leider suggest that the average person will change jobs seven to ten times during a lifetime.

- **Current Job Renewal:** Many people decide that their current job is actually a pretty good fit, and by "speaking up" for what they need they can get more of what they want from their current job and life circumstances and eliminate some of what they don't want. This is an excellent option, and is always the first step in improving your satisfaction at work.

Regardless of what you ultimately choose (career change, job change, or renewal), it is important that you not ignore signs that you are no longer satisfied with your work. The consequences of doing nothing can include poor performance, diminished self-esteem, depression, and even damage to your relationships with family and friends if you bring your unhappiness with work home with you (and this is almost inevitable).

Assessing Your Current Job

Directions: Write your answers to the following questions about your current job and how you feel about it.

1. At what stage are you in the life of your current job (new to the job, newness worn off, bored)?

2. What does it feel like to be at that stage (emotionally, physically)?

3. When have you been at this stage in a job before? What, if anything, did you do to stay challenged and productive?

4. If you are bored and "plateaued," which of the options (career, job change or renewal) are you currently considering? Why?

Current Job Renewal
(Individual Development Planning)

To make your career more satisfying, start with your current job. While this may not be what you want to hear, particularly if you dislike your current job, there are several reasons why this is true. First, your current job is available right now. Even if you decide today that you want to change jobs, it will take several months to find and start a new one. If you decide to change careers, it will probably take you a year or more. So, since you are likely to be in your current job for awhile, it makes sense to do what you can to make it more satisfying.

Second, your current job is the one you know best. No matter how well you research a new job, you cannot really know what it will be like until you have been in it for awhile. On the other hand, you already know the "goods" and the "bads" of your current job, and that puts you in a powerful position to change it for the better.

Third, **you will be a more attractive candidate for a new job if you are reasonably satisfied with your current job.** Employers are more eager to hire you when you are seeking a job because it fits well with your values, skills, and interests. They are much less eager to hire you if your primary reason for seeking a job is to leave a job you dislike. Staffing professionals say they can tell the difference in an interview, and that they view unhappy applicants with skepticism.

On the next several pages, you will work to complete an individual development plan for your current job. Specifically, you will be identifying ways to better use your talents, develop in areas that you need and want to improve, and make other changes in your work and perhaps outside of work to increase your satisfaction.

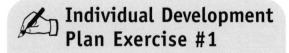

Using Your Talents More

Directions: Earlier, we defined talents as skills that come naturally to you, that are your "gifts," and that you enjoy using. One powerful strategy for increasing satisfaction in your current job is to identify and implement more ways to use your talents.

On page 36, you wrote a letter to your partner summarizing your skills and talents. Take a look at that letter again, and choose one talent which, if you could use it more in your current job, would increase your job satisfaction. Write it below.

Then, with the help of your partner, think of three ways you could better employ that talent in your job. For example, if you have a talent for writing, perhaps you could offer to start a company newsletter, or to help your boss with his or her correspondence. If your talent is performing, maybe you could take a more active role in your company meetings.

A word of caution: It is easy to confuse using a talent more often with getting better at it. The purpose of this exercise is not to think of ways to get better at a talent (so, for example, you probably don't need to take a class in your talent, unless that would be fun). The purpose of the exercise is to develop creative ideas for making your job more enjoyable by using your talents more.

Talent: _____

Ideas:

-
-
-
-
-

Learning New Skills (or Getting Better at Skills) Needed For Your Current Job

Directions: Another powerful strategy for increasing job satisfaction is to challenge yourself to learn or develop new skills. Often, the parts of a job that people like least are ones at which they feel least competent. Also, commiting yourself to building your competence at skills you are particularly interested in — and following through on that commitment — will build your confidence and self esteem and make your work more satisfying.

To identify skills you would like to enhance, consider these questions:

1. *Which skills do you and your boss agree are important to your job and are not currently your strengths? (If you need your boss to commit time and money toward your development, it makes sense to identify skills that benefit both you and your company.)*

2. *How could you develop those skills? (e.g. What classes does your company offer? What is your organization's policy on tuition reimbursement? Who do you know who is good at a skill you want to learn and might be willing to teach you? What books could you read?)*

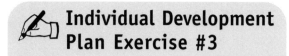

Other "Renewal" Strategies

Directions: Even if you can't change the content of your job much, there are still things you can do to "get off the plateau."

Listed below are ideas others have used successfully to "re-connect" with their enthusiasm for their life and work. Put a check next to ideas that appeal to you, and then add at least three other ideas that occur to you.

_____ *Begin to involve yourself in a new desired career (e.g. attend professional conferences, join a professional association in the new field and attend meetings, volunteer in an area of interest)*

_____ *Community involvement (chair a committee, teach a class, coach a sports team, etc.)*

_____ *Start a new hobby*

_____ *Spend more time with friends, colleagues, significant others, children*

_____ *Go back to school*

_____ *Become a mentor to someone*

_____

_____

_____

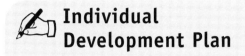 **Individual Development Plan**

Directions: On this page, you will use the work you completed in the previous three exercises to create an action plan for satisfaction and development in your current job.

Talents:

1. Which idea(s) for better using your talents are you committed to pursuing?

2. Whose support is necessary to implement your idea(s)?

3. What specific actions will you take, and by when?

■ *Action :*

By:_____

■ *Action:*

By:_____

Learning New Skills

1. What skill will you commit to building or enhancing?

2. Whose support is necessary?

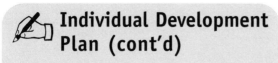

3. What specific actions will you take, and by when?

■ Action :

By:_____

■ Action:

By:_____

Other Renewal Strategies

1. What one or two actions could you take to implement your favorite idea?

2. What might prevent you from taking action? Who could help you move past your resistance?

Development Contracting

Once you have completed your action plan, meet with your partner and review your plan with him or her. Ask your partner to "sign off" on your plan. Knowing that someone else is expecting you to follow through will help you to stay commited to your plan.

You may also want to share your plan with your manager. He or she may be able to provide you with resources (time, money, etc.) to support your plan, and perhaps offer valuable feedback about your talents and about skills you need to improve. Your manager will also be able to do a better job of providing you with interesting, challenging work assignments if he or she knows what you are interested in.

Remember that gentleness is an important attitude when you are trying to make changes in your life. This applies both to you and to others who may resist your changes.

To help you to maintain an attitude of gentleness, and to focus your commitment, schedule a series of weekly telephone calls or face-to-face meetings for the next month with your partner to discuss your progress and frustrations as you implement your development plan. During these meetings, ask for support and honest feedback, and congratulate yourself for your hard work!

Section 4

Planning For Your Future

Section 4:
Planning For Your
Future

You may have reached a point in your job or career where, in addition to your efforts at increasing your current job satisfaction and effectiveness, you want to identify and begin work toward some long term career goals. For example, as a result of the self-discovery work you did earlier, you may have decided that you are satisfied with the career you have chosen, but want to identify your next job target. Or, you may have reached the conclusion that your current field no longer meets your needs, and you want to find a new career, but wonder how to act on that awareness.

Setting and achieving future career goals is, by necessity, a process of experimentation. Unfortunately, many people get stuck at this point because they want to be sure that the decisions and actions they take are the "right ones" before they take any action at all. The paradox is that, until you take action, you will not have the information you need to determine what a "successful" next step might be.

The way to get "unstuck" from this paradox is to recognize that the most important steps in setting and achieving future career goals include identifying **potential** next jobs or careers, and researching those options to see how well they might fit your values, skills, and interests. Informational interviewing and resume writing are two important strategies in this research process.

Notice that the word "potential" is highlighted in the previous paragraph. One of the exciting outcomes of this process is that as you research and talk with others about possible future goals, you will be presented with some totally new ideas.

The first step is to identify several possible jobs or careers and get started with your research and begin talking with people. The exercises on the following pages will help you do that.

Potential Next Job Exercise #1

Directions: Make a list of jobs (at least five) that you are interested in researching as possible future goals. These should be job titles (e.g. elementary school teacher, accountant, etc.) that are appealing. To help generate this list, consider the following questions:

1. *In our culture, envy is considered "bad." It can be useful, however, in learning to recognize your wants. When recently have you heard yourself say to yourself something like, "He/she is sure lucky" or "I could do that job!"? What jobs caused you to feel envious of someone?*

2. *The want-ads can be a useful resource for identifying jobs of interest. Go through the help wanted section of your Sunday newspaper. What jobs are appealing just because they sound interesting? (Note: Don't apply for the jobs, just notice which jobs interest you.)*

Job Titles:

1.

2.

3.

4.

5.

6.

7.

Potential Next Job
Exercise #2

Directions:

A) Write down your three top values and five favorite skills on the worksheet below. Also, write down three of your interests.(Refer back to Section 2 of the workbook on pages 26, 31 and 37).

B) Then, take five copies of this two-page worksheet and give one each to five people whose input you value and ask them to write down the names of five jobs that they think would satisfy your values, skills, and interests.

C) Use the suggestions you get back and the ideas you generated in Potential Job Exercise #1 to complete the worksheet on page 58.

My top three values:

1.

2.

3.

My favorite skills to use in a job:

1.

2.

3

4.

5.

My three interests:

1.

2.

3.

Five jobs that would satisfy my values, skills, and interests:

1.

2.

3.

4.

5.

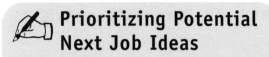

Prioritizing Potential Next Job Ideas

Directions: You probably have more ideas than you can handle after the previous exercises. Now, take all of the ideas and prioritize them according to the following criteria:

First priority: Begin to research now (no more than five ideas)

Second priority: Explore only after you have researched and eliminated all of the first priority ideas

Maybe later (or hobbies): Low priority ideas (of little interest) or ideas that might suggest new hobbies but not career interests

Researching Potential Next Jobs

Now that you have some ideas about possible next jobs, how do you start to research them?

Your Local Library

Go to your local library. Ask the librarian for resources for learning about the characteristics and training required for various jobs. Some useful reference sources include:

- *Dictionary of Occupational Titles*
- *Occupational Outlook Handbook*
- Trade publications in your field of interest
- Annual reports of companies which interest you
- Business section of your local newspaper

The Internet

In recent years, a huge quantity of websites have become available to help with career planning. You can find a variety of self-assessments, help with resume writing, tools for researching various types of jobs, job openings, opportunities to send your resume to potential employers, and other help and advice. Spending time finding and exploring the various sites is enjoyable and rewarding.

However, a word of caution is in order. Research suggests that only a small percentage of job seekers actually get hired as a result of applying for jobs via the Web. Most good jobs are found through personal relationships, and thus there is simply no substitute for networking and informational interviewing.

Informational Interviewing

The most important way to research next job possibilities is via informational interviewing. The article starting on the next page provides an excellent overview of informational interviewing, including the purpose, identifying someone to interview, how to request the informational interview, preparing for and conducting the interview, and following up after the interview.

Informational Interviews

The Purpose

Informational interviews are an excellent research tool for investigating occupational options. These interviews are used by many individuals to obtain the information needed to make informed career choices. From a consumer standpoint, it makes sense to get the facts about an occupation before you invest time and money pursuing it. Keep in mind that you will probably want to interview several people in order to get a balanced picture of what it's like to work in various settings.

An informational interview can provide you with the opportunity to meet and talk with someone who is working in or is knowledgeable about an occupation that you are considering. If possible, arrange to conduct the interview at the person's place of employment so that you can also get a feel for the organization and the work environment.

Identifying Someone to Interview

When you identify an occupational area to explore, try using your personal or professional network to identify appropriate people to contact. Since many people feel somewhat apprehensive at the thought of contacting "strangers," referrals from people you know may help to get you started.

Call people you already know and tell them that you are interested in learning more about a specific job. Ask if they know anyone working in this area who might be willing to talk with you or if they have any ideas about how you could meet someone doing this kind of work. Thank them for their assistance. Follow up on all leads.

If your network doesn't produce at least one name to get you started, try contacting professional associations, educational or training programs, or employing organizations. The Yellow Pages, professional publications and directories, business magazines and newsletters, and the daily newspaper are all particularly helpful in identifying someone to interview. People often feel complimented to be contacted and asked to talk about themselves and their work, especially when they hear that you learned about them while researching the occupation.

Requesting the Interview

Once you identify the person you want to talk with, call to request an interview at a convenient time and place. Suggest conducting the interview where the person works.

Prepare a script of what you want to say and practice making the call before you actually make it. Include the following information:

- Your name

- How you got the person's name

- Your reason for calling — exploring a career change, investigating career options

- Your goal — to arrange an informational interview

Many individuals are familiar with informational interviews and have conducted these interviews themselves. If someone seems unfamiliar with informational interviews, you can easily explain your purpose: You are interested in learning more about the work they do and would like to set up a time to meet with them.

Have your calendar available and write down the date, time, address and specific directions. Give the person your name and phone number in case it becomes necessary to reschedule.

Note: Remember that your purpose in conducting an informational interview is to obtain information about an occupation. Although you need to conduct it just as professionally as a job interview, it is not a job interview.

Preparing for the Interview

If you do some background reading about the occupation prior to the interview, you will make better use of the interview time. Identify specific questions that cannot be easily answered elsewhere. The OOH (Occupational Outlook Handbook) provides a comprehensive overview for many occupations. Other helpful resources are available in the career and business reference sections of libraries. Ask a reference librarian to help you identify appropriate materials.

Conducting the Interview

Dress appropriately (as you would for a job interview) and arrive on time in order to make a good impression. Prepare specific questions about the field. Stick to the agreed-upon time limit unless the person you are interviewing volunteers to spend more time with you. Ask permission to take a few notes, e.g., names of people, organizations, publications or training programs that you learn about. Do not make notes of confidential information. Ask if it is possible to tour the work site.

Following the Interview

As soon as possible after the interview, write up your notes and impressions for future reference. Include both factual information and your reactions to what you learned about the occupation and the person you interviewed. After several interviews it often becomes difficult to remember everything you learned and to keep your source straight.

Always send a personalized thank-you note after the interview. In it mention at least one thing which was particularly helpful or on which you plan to follow up. Thank the person for taking the time to meet with you.

Author Unknown

Examples of Questions for an Informational Interview

- What is your job title? Does this position also go by other job titles?

- What is the typical day/week like for you?

- How many hours do you routinely work? Are you on a set schedule? Are you required to work irregular hours (overtime, weekends, evenings, holidays)?

- What skills and personal characteristics are necessary to be successful in this occupation?

- How much freedom do you have to decide how to perform your work?

- How did you obtain your position?

- What is your educational background?

- What do you like most about your work? What do you like least?

- What are the greatest sources of stress associated with your job?

- What career options does this position provide?

- What other types of organizations employ people in this field?

- Are there related occupations that I might also want to explore?

- What recommendations do you have for someone who would like to enter this field now?

- What academic preparation is desirable? Indispensable? What experience is desirable? Indispensable?

- What courses/experience are most valuable in order to gain the skills needed in this occupation?

- What kinds of experience and credentials (degree, certificate, license) do employers look for when hiring for this position?

- What steps are necessary to break into this occupation?

- How competitive is entry into this field?

- What is the employment outlook for this field?

- What is the salary range for entry-level positions?

- What are the opportunities for advancement? To which positions? Is an advanced degree needed? In what?

- What professional publications do people in this field read?

- To what professional organizations do people in this field belong?

- Given what I've told you about my skills and background, is it realistic for me to consider moving into this field?

- Who do you suggest I talk to for additional information? May I use your name as a reference?

- Do you think I left out any important questions?

Informational Interviewing Plan

It is hard to over-emphasize the importance of informational interviewing. It is by actually talking to people who are doing jobs that you are interested in, that you "reality test" the work that you have been doing up to this point.

Informational interviewing is helpful in many ways:

- It will energize and excite you to talk to people about your future.

- You will gain confidence and skill at meeting with others and at asking and answering questions. This will improve your interviewing skills for future job opportunities.

- You may discover that you would not like the particular job you are researching. It is much better to find this out early before you commit a lot of time and energy to pursuing the job.

- You may discover new job opportunities that you had never thought of before.

- You will make useful contacts for the future.

- You may discover that your current job is better than you thought, and that staying put and working on renewal is your best strategy.

Getting started with informational interviewing can be a little intimidating, particularly if you have not done it before. You can start by interviewing a friend or two to get comfortable with calling and asking for an interview, and to practice asking questions.

Some tips to help your interviews go smoothly:

- **Before making your first call, take a few minutes and write down what you will say to ask for the interviewing opportunity.** You might say something like, "I am exploring some options for future career goals for myself, and would like to learn more about what your job is like. Would you be willing to meet with me for about 30 minutes to answer some questions I have?"

- **Prepare your questions in advance.** In the interview, you want to find out whether the job you are researching will fit with your values, use your favorite skills, and provide work that interests you. Refer back to the suggested questions at the end of the previous article on informational interviewing and select five or six questions that will get at the information you need. During the interview, feel free to ask additional questions that come to mind.

- **At the end of each interview, ask the interviewee if they can suggest others to contact.** This will broaden your network of contacts. Also, thank the interviewee for taking the time to talk with you.

Informational Interviewing Plan

Directions: In the first column, write the names of the jobs you want to explore. In the second column, write down the name and telephone number of one or two people you could call to interview about each job. In the third column, set a date by which you will call to request an interview.

Job	*Name, Phone #*	*By when*
1.	■	
	■	
2.	■	
	■	
3.	■	
	■	
4.	■	
	■	
5.	■	
	■	

Writing a Resume

After doing a few informational interviews, you will probably find it helpful to have a resume to leave with the person you have interviewed.

Keep in mind that a resume will not "sell you" or get you a job. Only you can do that. However, a resume does serve some important purposes:

- The process of writing a resume helps you to organize your own understanding of your career objective and how your past experience relates to your objective.

- It gives you something tangible to leave behind after an informational interview or to attach to a follow-up note.

- It provides information about you to assist the person in preparation for your informational interview.

Parts of a Resume

Most resumes include the following five parts:

- **The Objective:** The type of job you want

- **Highlights of Qualifications:** Key experiences, credentials, accomplishments, skills

- **Employment History:** Brief chronological work history

- **Relevant Skills and Experience:** Examples of how you have used the key skills required for your job objective

- **Education and Training:** Relevant education and training

It is beyond the scope of this workbook to provide you with specific instructions for writing your resume. Go to your local library and find a resume-writing guide to help you. The best guides present samples that you can use as a reference. I would recommend:

- *The Damn Good Résumé Guide,* by Yana Parker, Ten Speed Press, 1983

- *How to Write Better Resumes,* by Gary Joseph Grappo and Adele Lewis, Barron's, 1998

You can find many good resources on the Internet, and there are many software programs available to help with resume writing. Using your personal computer, you can easily customize your resume for different situations (e.g. you may want to highlight different experiences depending on the type of job you are exploring). There are also professionals who specialize in creating resumes, and their expertise can be invaluable.

One final caution: **Do not use writing a resume as an excuse for putting off informational interviewing.** In the long run, the contacts you make and the information you gather through informational interviewing will be far more important in accomplishing your future goals.

Changing Jobs or Careers

The end result of your informational interviewing and other research efforts is to identify a new job or career as a future goal. Now comes the next challenge — turning your goals into reality.

The specific steps required to realize your goals will be different for each person. It may require going back to school to build new knowledge and skills. It may require making a "lateral" move or even starting at a "lower" level than your current job in order to eventually end up where you want to be.

Flexibility, curiosity, a willingness to learn new skills, and strong self-respect are critical assets to carry with you as you embark on your path. The experience of others who have traveled the same path will also be very useful.

Listed below are some "tips," based on others' experience, to help make you the best possible candidate for future career opportunities.

- I perform well in my current position.

- I have researched personal skills/values in advance to be able to recognize appropriate job matches.

- I apply for positions that truly are a "fit" rather than only those with higher grade-level/salary. I do not apply for new jobs merely to "jump-ship."

- I recognize and understand that lateral movement and even accepting a new position at a lower grade level is sometimes beneficial and necessary for long-term career development.

- I bring a positive attitude to my current job and my request for a job change.

- I approach the internal job posting process with the same competitive edge as if I were applying for an external position.

- I am professional. I complete the job application neatly and accurately. My resume is up-to-date and error free. At the interview, I dress appropriately, am timely and prepared.

- I show follow-through. I send a thank-you note after each interview.

- Above all, I do not get discouraged. I put my best foot forward and continue to take proactive steps to develop my skills and interests.

Moving Forward

An old saying goes, "If nothing changes, nothing changes." This is certainly true of jobs and careers. For many, one of the biggest challenges in making their work more satisfying is the fear and discomfort they encounter when they begin to take proactive steps to change. This fear and discomfort is a sign of resistance, which is the topic of *Section 5: The Challenge of Change.*

Section 5

The Challenge of Change

Section 5:
The Challenge
of Change

Resistance and Habitual Thinking

Since you persevered to this point in the workbook, you deserve tremendous credit. To get here you asked yourself many hard questions, and you took action in ways that were perhaps initially difficult and scary.

In conclusion, stop to consider resistance and habitual thinking, two roadblocks to new growth and change in your life. Resistance has to do with fear: fear of being judged inadequate, fear of being embarrassed. Habitual thinking refers to your typical ways of viewing and responding to the world. Throughout your life, you have learned ways of thinking about how life is and how it should be, and it can be difficult to alter these habits.

A lot of the difficulty in making changes in your life, even positive changes, relates to resistance and habitual thinking. The classic example is making New Year's resolutions, such as starting to exercise or lose weight, only to fall back into old patterns by January 15. New ways of thinking and acting "run into" old beliefs and patterns of thought about the world, and often the old habits "win."

In her book *The Wisdom of No Escape*, Pema Chodron writes: "The problem is that the desire to change is fundamentally a form of aggression towards yourself. The other problem is that our hang-ups, unfortunately or fortunately, contain our wealth." In this context, fear and resistance to change make sense. All of us resist "acts of aggression." And, all of us resist giving up our "wealth."

So what is the answer to this dilemma? Chodron goes on to say: "The innocent mistake that keeps us caught in our own particular style of ignorance ... is that **we are never encouraged to see clearly what is, with gentleness** [my emphasis]. Instead, there is a basic misunderstanding that we should try to be better than we already are, that we should try to improve ourselves ...."

So, should you not try to change? We can be accepting of what we learn, and then **gently** try new behaviors of our choosing, not those forced upon us.

Five Qualities of Empowerment

In his book *Even Eagles Need a Push,* David McNally suggests that confident, empowered individuals need to cultivate five qualities. These qualities are embodied in the work you have done in the **Taking Charge of Your Career** workbook:

1. *Vision:* The ability to articulate your goals and aspirations for the future

2. *Self-Appreciation:* Knowing who you are; your values, your interests, your skills, and appreciating your basic goodness

3. *Purpose:* Having a reason beyond yourself for living and working

4. **Commitment:** A willingness to move through resistance and habitual thinking in order to achieve your goals

5. **Contribution:** Thinking in terms of *giving,* not just in terms of getting

This workbook began by saying that old ways of thinking about why we work, and what creates meaning, motivation, and satisfaction at work, are no longer useful. Charles Darwin said, "It is not the strongest of the species that survives, nor the most intelligent, but rather the most responsive to change." By completing this workbook, you have demonstrated your responsiveness. Congratulations on your efforts and commitment to **Taking Charge of Your Career**.

Section 6

Appendix:
Guide for Facilitators and Career Coaches

Section 6:
Appendix: Guide
for Facilitators and
Career Coaches

The **Taking Charge of Your Career** workbook is based on a workshop of the same name that has been successfully offered in organizations throughout the United States during the past ten years. Consequently, the workbook can be used as a self-directed learning tool, or as a participant workbook for a facilitated workshop in career and personal development.

The **Taking Charge of Your Career** workshop can be offered in a variety of formats including a one-day session, two one-half-day sessions, or four two-hour-long sessions. One of the benefits of this flexibility in format is that you can customize the workshop to meet the scheduling requirements of your clients. A second major advantage is that the workshop offers the option to add organization-specific content to the core workshop. In this way, you can create a "customized" version that is unique to your organization.

For example, some organizations add specific content on their internal job posting program, educational reimbursement programs, and other development policies and practices. Others have included employee panels from different parts of their organization to educate participants on various career options offered within the organization.

Another common addition to the workshop, if the organization has a qualified practitioner on staff or available as a consultant, is to offer assessments such as the Myers-Briggs Type Indicator® or Strong Interest Inventory™ to augment the exercises in the **Taking Charge of Your Career** workbook.

Workshop Design

The basic design of the **Taking Charge of Your Career** workshop follows closely the organization of the workbook. Starting on the next page is the outline for the workshop when it is divided into two sessions, each one-half day in length.

Taking Charge of Your Career Workshop

Session 1 (One-half day)

8:00 Welcome, purpose of the session, facilitator and participant introductions

8:30 Small group analysis of the case study about Mary (pages 8-9) with large group de-brief which includes information from *Section 1: Career Development Fundamentals*

9:25 Break

9:35 Career Aspirations Dialogue (pages 16-19) and de-brief

10:45 Overview of *Section 2: Learning About Your Work Self*

11:00 Values Clarification Exercise (Identify top values from pages 27-28) and answer the questions in Values Exercise #2 (page 28); discuss results in small groups

11:40 Overview other self knowledge exercises and bibliography

11:55 Assign homework for Session 2

- Review *Section 3: Assessing Your Current Job* and *Section 4: Planning For Your Future*

- Complete selected additional exercises from *Section 2: Learning About Your Work Self* (e.g. skills exercise, interests exercise)

12:00 End of Session 1

Session 2 (One-half day)

8:00 Check-in on learnings from Session 1

8:30 Discussion of Current Job Assessment Model (pages 42-43) and discussion of the questions on page 44 in small groups

9:00 Quick lecturette on Individual Development Planning (page 45)

9:15 Participants complete Individual Development Plan Exercises #1 and #2 (pages 46-47) and, time permitting, the Individual Development Plan (pages 49-50)

9:55 Break

10:05 Informational Interviewing (page 60)

10:20 Informational Interviewing Practice (participants pair up and practice interviewing each other)

10:55 Quick input on resume writing (pages 66-67)

11:10 Discuss Making a Job Change checklist (page 68)

11:30* Action Planning and next steps

11:55 Evaluations and Close

*I often rent and show the video *Even Eagles Need a Push*, which is available from CRM Films (1-800-421-0833), as a way to end the workshop on a "high" note.

The two sessions can be combined into a full-day session, or further divided into four two-hour sessions.

If you would like more information about the **Taking Charge of Your Career** Workshop, please e-mail us at:

The Bailey Consulting Group
lbailey@thebaileygroup.com

Meeting 4: Future Planning

Use Potential Next Job Exercise #1 (page 55) to facilitate a discussion of future career goals and actions required to achieve these goals.

Discuss informational interviewing as a tool for researching jobs that are of interest to your client (pages 60-64). Work with the client to begin the Informational Interviewing Plan (page 65).

Have your client try an informational interview with you as a way to build confidence.

Assignment: If your client is having a hard time coming up with future job possibilities, have them complete Potential Next Job Exercise #2 (pages 56-57). Also, have the client try an informational interview with a friend to get more practice and continue to build confidence.

Meeting 5: Wrap Up

Discuss the uses of resumes and the parts of a resume. Suggest resources for help in writing a resume (pages 64-65).

Discuss the Changing Jobs or Careers Checklist (page 68) and resistance to change (pages 72-73).

Contract for future meetings as needed.

The above is one suggested approach to using the **Taking Charge of Your Career** workbook to support your career coaching. Obviously, you should feel free to develop your own approach and to augment the workbook with other materials that you have found to be helpful.

For more information, contact Leigh Bailey at lbailey@thebaileygroup.com.

Bibliography

Bailey, Leigh, *Taking Charge of Your Career, Revised Edition*, Golden Valley, MN: The Bailey Consulting Group, 2002.

Bolles, Richard, *The New Quick Job Hunting Map*, Berkeley, CA: Ten Speed Press, 1990.

Bridges, William, *Transitions*, Reading, MA: Addision-Wesley Publishing Co., 1980.

Briggs Myers, Isabel, *Introduction to Type*, Palo Alto, CA: Consulting Psychologists Press, 1962.

Cameron, Julia, *The Artist's Way*, New York, NY: The Putnam Publishing Group, 1992.

Chödrön, Pema, *The Wisdom of No Escape and the Path of Loving-Kindness*, Boston, MA: Shambhala Publications, 1991.

Dunning, Donna, *What's Your Type of Career? Unlock the Secrets of Your Personality to Find Your Perfect Career Path*, Palo Alto, CA: Davies-Black Publishing, 2001.

Figler, Howard, *The Complete Job Search Handbook*, New York: Henry Holt and Company, 1988.

Frankel, Viktor E., *Man's Search for Meaning*, New York: Washington Square Press, 1973.

Gruppo, Gary and Lewis, Adele, *How to Write Better Resumes (Fifth Edition)*, Hauppage, NY: Barrons, 1998.

Hagberg, Janet and Leider, Richard, *The Inventurers*, Reading, MA: Addison-Wesley Publishing, Co., 1978.

Hanson, K. & Hanson, R., *Dynamic Cover Letters*, Berkeley, CA: Ten Speed Press, 1990.

Kaye, Beverly and Jordan-Evans, Sharon, *Love 'Em or Lose 'Em: Getting Good People to Stay*, San Francisco, CA: Berrett-Koehler Publishers, Inc., 1999.

Leider, Richard J. and Shapiro, David A., *Repacking Your Bags: Lighten Your Load for the Rest of Your Life*, San Francisco, CA: Berrett-Koehler Publishers, Inc., 1995, 1996.

Leider, Richard J. and Shapiro, David A., *Whistle While You Work: Heeding Your Life's Calling*, San Francisco, CA: Berrett-Koehler Publishers, Inc., 2001.

McNally, David, *Even Eagles Need a Push*, New York, New York: Delacorte Press, 1991.

Medley, H. Anthony, *Sweaty Palms — The Neglected Art of Being Interviewed*, Berkeley, CA: Ten Speed Press, 1992.

Parker, Yana, *The Damn Good Résumé Guide*, Berkeley, CA: Ten Speed Press, 1989.

Sher, Barbara, *Wishcraft: How to Get What You Really Want*, New York: Ballentine Books, 1979.

Tieger, Paul and Barron-Tieger, Barbara, *Do What You Are*, Boston, MIT: Little, Brown and Company, 1992.